D1064584

in
the
news™

STARVATION IN AFRICA

Linley Erin Hall

ROSEN
PUBLISHING®

New York

Published in 2007 by The Rosen Publishing Group, Inc.
29 East 21st Street, New York, NY 10010

First Edition

Library of Congress Cataloging-in-Publication Data

Hall, Linley Erin.
Starvation in Africa / Linley Erin Hall.
     p. cm.—(In the news)
Includes bibliographical references and index.
ISBN-13: 978-1-4042-0976-3
ISBN-10: 1-4042-0976-X (library binding)
1. Famines—Africa. 2. Food supply—Africa. 3. Famines—Africa—History. 4. Africa—Economic conditions—1960– I. Title.
HC800.Z9F343 2007
363.8096—dc22
                                                          2006020876

Manufactured in the United States of America

On the cover: Top right: A parched riverbed in East Africa. Top left: A Malawian woman carries a sack of maize provided by the World Food Programme. Bottom: An Ethiopian child suffering from malnutrition.

contents

1 **Geography and History of Famine**
   in Africa   **4**

2 **Elements of Famine**   **17**

3 **Twentieth-Century African Famines**   **30**

4 **Current Famines in Africa**   **40**

5 **Strategies to Combat Famine**   **48**

Glossary   **56**

For More Information   **57**

For Further Reading   **59**

Bibliography   **60**

Index   **63**

Geography and History of Famine in Africa

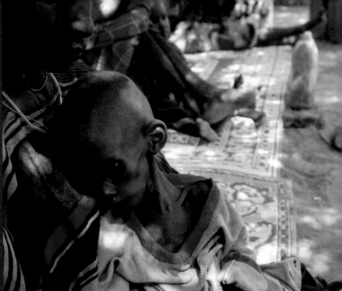

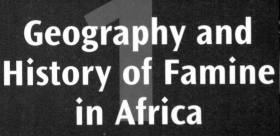

People who are under-nourished lack enough of the proper food for good health and development. According to the United Nations World Food Programme (WFP), approximately 800 million people in the world are undernourished. This is 16 percent of the world's population. The United Nations Children's Fund (UNICEF) estimates that undernourishment contributes to the deaths of 5.6 million children under the age of five each year.

Most people who are undernourished live in

developing countries. In these areas, many people don't earn a lot of money, and there isn't a lot of industry. Developing countries also score poorly on the United Nations' Human Development Index, which measures life expectancy, poverty, education, literacy, childbirth, and other factors that contribute to well-being.

In May 2006, the United Nations Food and Agriculture Organization (FAO) announced that thirty-nine countries were currently facing food shortages. Twenty-four of these were in Africa. On the Human Development Index, eighteen of these countries are least developed nations with scores of less than 0.5 (on a scale of 0 to 1).

Undernourishment, hunger, and famine have plagued Africa for decades. A famine is a wide-reaching shortage of food that leaves many people hungry, even starving. Many organizations and nations avoid using the word "famine" unless the problem is very widespread and long-lasting. They may instead refer to a "food crisis" or "food shortage." Whatever it is called, the result is the same: people without enough to eat and in failing health.

According to the United Nations World Food Programme (WFP), approximately 800 million people in the world are undernourished. This is 16 percent of the world's population. The United Nations Children's Fund (UNICEF) estimates that undernourishment contributes to the deaths of 5.6 million children under the age of five each year.

The world contains more than enough food to feed everyone. The food is distributed unevenly, however, and doesn't always get to where it's most needed. In an attempt to address this problem, representatives from 180 nations met in Rome, Italy, in 1996 for the United Nations World Food Summit. They issued the Rome Declaration on World Food Security. This declaration included the goal of reducing the number of undernourished people to half its 1996 level by the year 2015. In September 2000, government leaders met in New York City for the United Nations Millennium Summit. There, they drafted the Millennium Declaration. This document contains humanitarian and development-related goals for the world in many different areas. It also repeats the Rome Declaration's goal of halving world hunger by 2015.

Unfortunately, the world is not on track to meet that goal. Africa, in particular, lags behind. According to UNICEF, between 1990 and 2004 the proportion of underweight children in developing nations decreased from 33 to 28 percent. Most of the progress occurred in Asia and Latin America; the percentage of underweight children in sub-Saharan Africa remained about the same. In fact, since the African population grew, the number of underweight kids there actually increased.

A large number of people in Africa are hungry for many different reasons. Chronic hunger in Africa is caused by various economic, social, political, and environmental conditions, many of them interrelated in a complex web of intensifying cause and effect. This book examines the history, causes, and potential solutions for food crises in Africa and around the world.

The Geography of Africa

Africa is a huge continent that encompasses fifty-four countries. Geography, religious beliefs, cultural traditions, history, and politics vary widely from country to country. This chapter looks at the geography and history of Africa as they relate to agriculture and food crises.

The African continent includes fifty-four countries divided into several regions.

Africa is often divided into two regions, North Africa and sub-Saharan Africa. North Africa encompasses much of the Sahara Desert and the non-desert areas on the Mediterranean Sea. North African nations are often more culturally, economically, and politically tied to the Middle East and to Europe than to other countries in Africa.

Sub-Saharan Africa is all of Africa south of the Sahara Desert. Two major geographic bands run horizontally across sub-Saharan Africa. The Sahel is a band of land that stretches across the African continent. It is located between the Sahara Desert to the north and the Sudan region to the south. The Sudan region is a strip of land that also reaches much of the way across Africa. Both the Sahel and the Sudan are savanna (dry, mostly treeless plains that contain drought-resistant grasslands), although the Sudan receives more rain. South of the Sudan are wet tropical forests that give way to drier regions and then the deserts of southern Africa.

In tropical areas, rain falls in all months, sometimes up to 120 inches (304.8 centimeters) per year. Regions north and south of the tropical forests have alternating wet seasons and dry seasons. Usually, rainfall is either too much or too little. It's rarely just right. Temperatures are warm. In tropical areas, the average temperature in the coldest month is 64 degrees Fahrenheit (17.8 degrees Celsius). The land never freezes; there is no frost, no snow, and no ice.

Lack of frost should be a benefit to farmers. They should be able to grow more crops on the same land during a year-round growing season, since cold temperatures won't kill the plants. But the soil in many parts of Africa does not contain many nutrients. Tropical soils replenish their nutrients from dead organic matter such

Africa contains deserts, tropical forests, and savanna in different areas. Each environment poses different food supply challenges.

as fallen leaves and trees. When forests are cleared for farming, this replenishment is often lost. In addition, the long dry seasons interspersed with wet seasons make growing many crops difficult.

Africa can also be divided according to region. The United Nations groups Africa into the regions of West Africa, East Africa, Central Africa, and southern Africa. Countries in these regions often have more in common with each other than with nations in other parts of Africa.

In a few cases, the same name is used for different entities. For example, the name Sahel is often used to refer to the six countries in West Africa that contain part of the Sahel. These are Mauritania, Senegal, Mali, Burkina Faso, Niger, and Chad. This book will use the term "Sahelian countries" to refer to these nations. There is also a country named Sudan. It contains part of the Sudan geographic region, but not all of it. In this book, "the Sudan" will refer to the geographic region, and "Sudan" to the country.

History

Throughout history, African societies have adapted to their often-extreme environment and climate. For example, many African tribes moved according to the seasons. This is known as a nomadic existence. A pastoralist is someone who raises livestock by moving between several different pastures that offer his or her animals food during different times of the year. In eastern Sudan, the Hadenowa people planted sorghum near rivers. Then they took their camels to wet-season pastures far away. Eight months later, they returned when the sorghum was ready to harvest.

Traditional Agricultural Practices

Some farmers in tropical areas practiced "shifting." This means that they chopped down the forest to create a field, used the field for a few years until the soil's nutrients were depleted, and then moved on. The original field was taken over by forest again. This replaced nutrients in the soil that farming had used up. Shifting made sure that the land was never completely depleted of nutrients and thus unusable for either farming or forest.

Other societies remained in one place. These people planted carefully, timing the planting and growing seasons with the seasonal rains. Their farming practices made careful use of the nutrients in the soil. Many different crops were grown in small patches alternating with one another. Acres of teff, a kind of wheat, might be planted between acres of yams. Farmers rotated crops, not growing the same thing in the same field twice in a row. They also left some fields unused, or fallow. Crop rotation and fallow fields guard against completely removing nutrients from the soil.

Alternating crops (planting different crops in adjacent fields) also helps protect against pests and weeds. Many insects prefer to eat only certain plants. For example, one acre of corn might become infested with weevils. The weevils are unlikely to spread to other acres of corn, however, because they would have to traverse acres of yams or other crops, which they don't like to eat. The entire corn crop isn't lost as a result of crop alternation.

In some parts of Africa, these techniques for farming and raising livestock are still used today. But contact with non-Africans changed farming practices in many areas, temporarily or permanently, and often for the worse.

The Slave Trade

The slave trade in Africa dates back to the first century AD. When tribespeople were captured during wars with rival tribes, they were often used as slaves. Tribes began to sell slaves to foreigners—mostly Europeans and the European colonies of the Americas—in return for a variety of goods. This slave trade increased considerably in the last half of the eighteenth century. The primary buyers were the British, Portuguese, French, and Spanish. These countries needed laborers for their vast plantations in the Americas. Northeast Africa, Arabia, and Persia also bought slaves.

The slave trade encouraged tribes to war with each other for the explicit purpose of capturing prisoners to sell as slaves. Tribal leaders used the profits from selling slaves to obtain horses and guns. They also invested in defensive walls and foreign goods. The money wasn't generally used to expand or improve agriculture, although contact with Europeans introduced new plants to Africa. Slaves were traded for maize, sweet potatoes, and cassava. Once foreign, these crops are now essential in some parts of Africa.

Raids of enemy tribes by slave traders meant that many people fled for their lives and hid in the jungle.

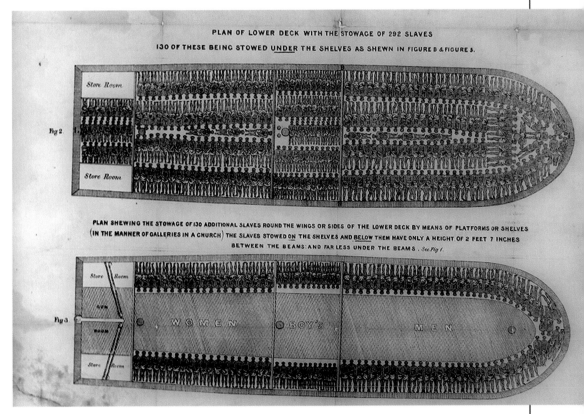

PLAN OF LOWER DECK WITH THE STOWAGE OF 292 SLAVES
130 OF THESE BEING STOWED UNDER THE SHELVES AS SHEWN IN FIGURE D & FIGURE 5.

PLAN SHEWING THE STOWAGE OF 130 ADDITIONAL SLAVES ROUND THE WINGS OR SIDES OF THE LOWER DECK BY MEANS OF PLATFORMS OR SHELVES (IN THE MANNER OF GALLERIES IN A CHURCH) THE SLAVES STOWED ON THE SHELVES AND BELOW THEM HAVE ONLY A HEIGHT OF 2 FEET 7 INCHES BETWEEN THE BEAMS: AND FAR LESS UNDER THE BEAMS. See Fig 1.

In the eighteenth and nineteenth centuries, huge ships transported slaves from Africa to the Americas. The slave trade disrupted agriculture in Africa, in some cases causing food crises.

Their deserted farmland led to a decrease in food production. Slave traders also destroyed many crops during their rampages. Though European nations abolished the slave trade in the early 1800s, it continued in some areas until the early 1900s.

Colonialism

During the height of the slave trade, Europeans were starting to explore the African continent. In the late

1800s, the major European powers competed with each other to control parts of the continent. Great Britain, France, Italy, Belgium, Germany, and Portugal all established colonies in Africa. Colonies are territories that typically are ruled by a distant mother country.

Europeans began to introduce Western agriculture to their African colonies. Huge fields were planted with the same crop. This allowed pests (like locusts) and weeds to spread easily, often destroying the entire crop. As a result, more labor and technological inputs such as fertilizer and pesticides were required to make these crops successful. In addition, they were cash crops planted not for local use and nourishment, but for export and use by the mother country. Often, these crops were not food at all but other agricultural products, like cotton.

In some cases, conflicts between colonial rulers and the local people led to famine. For example, the Maji Maji uprising in Tanzania occurred from 1905 to 1907. The locals revolted against forced labor in the cotton fields. An estimated 75,000 Africans died in the subsequent war and famine.

Continuing Western Influence Following Independence

Most African colonies lasted less than 100 years. In the 1950s and 1960s, most African nations achieved independence from their mother countries. But the new national boundaries were generally based on the colonial

Carol Bellamy *(right)*, executive director of UNICEF, visits Somalia in 2000. Organizations such as UNICEF are working to end food crises in Africa.

boundaries drawn by European nations. This meant that many different ethnic and religious groups are likely to be part of one country, and they don't necessarily get along. Many African nations have been involved in armed conflicts, often civil wars within their borders. These conflicts impact food production in many ways.

Western nations have tried to help African countries to develop and industrialize. The United Nations, the

World Bank, and other agencies have provided money and support for projects such as dams, roads, and factories. African nations have also been encouraged to expand the planting of cash crops. Loans have been made to modernize agriculture through the use of tractors, fertilizers, pesticides, and other tools. Cash crops are often grown on the best land in a nation. Peasant farmers and pastoralists have been relocated to land that isn't as rich and productive. This increases the possibility that their crops—grown for local nourishment and sustenance—will fail.

These Western efforts to modernize African nations have not always been offered free of charge. Many African countries have huge debts. A debt is money that is owed to someone else. In 1970, African debt to non-African nations and organizations was very small. But by the early 1990s, it had ballooned to more than $200 billion. Often, much of the money that a country makes by exporting cash crops and other items must go toward repaying its debts. In this sense, some African nations never have the chance to get ahead; at best, they just keep running in place.

This disruption of traditional agricultural practices has set the stage for repeated, widespread food crises in Africa.

Elements of Famine

A term that is often used in relation to the agricultural and distribution policies of developing countries is "food security." It's achieved when all people always have access to enough nutritious and safe food. Food security involves four components. First, the food supply must be adequate to feed everyone. Second, the food supply cannot change drastically from season to season or year to year. Third, the food must be accessible and affordable. Fourth, the food must be safe and of good quality.

Many countries in Africa experience tremendous food insecurity, rather than food security. When drought, war, or other factors decrease the amount of food a country produces, many citizens cannot be fed. Many will experience extreme, prolonged hunger, and some will even starve to death. Developing countries often do not have adequate food reserves. They also don't have enough money to buy extra food in famine emergencies. This can easily lead to a food crisis.

Different things contribute to food insecurity, under-nutrition, and famine in Africa. Many causes of famine are also the results of famine. This can set up a vicious cycle in which conditions continue to get worse, or at least not get any better. Some of the factors that contribute to—and can be worsened and intensified by—famine will be examined here.

Climate

In Africa, crops are more affected by changes in rainfall than by changes in temperature. A drought is an extended period of time with little or no rain. During a drought, the soil becomes very dry. Nutrient-rich topsoil may blow away in the wind. Crops grow poorly, or not at all, during a drought.

Many parts of Africa have wet seasons and dry seasons. The rains can arrive early or late, or fall for a longer or shorter time than usual. This can have a huge impact on harvests. For example, the rains may seem to start, causing people to plant their seeds. If the rains stop quickly, however, a second planting may be necessary when the rains truly begin. Buying new seed can be expensive, and replanting is time-consuming. In recent decades, droughts have become more frequent and severe in some parts of Africa.

A Nigerian farmer works in a cornfield. Drought in African nations is a major cause of famine.

Farming Techniques and Overuse of Land

Most farmland in Africa relies only on rain for water. Irrigation provides water to some fields through ditches or pipes. This water usually comes from rivers, lakes, or other bodies of water. Irrigation can provide water to fields when rain is scarce. But poorly used irrigation can cause erosion.

Erosion occurs when soil is removed by wind or water. Excess water from over-irrigation or heavy rain can carry the soil away. The wind may also blow it away during a drought. Removing plants whose root systems help keep the soil in place can allow erosion to happen faster.

Erosion has damaged some of the farmland in Africa. The continent's tropical soils do not contain very many nutrients. Erosion and poor farming practices quickly remove these nutrients. This makes the land unproductive. Using fertilizer can put important nutrients back into the soil. Chemical fertilizers are expensive, however. They can also pollute the water supply with chemicals that are harmful to fish, humans, and other living things.

When people fear hunger, they are more likely to use land inappropriately and over-farm it. This can provide more food in the short term. In the long term, however, the environment is harmed, the soil is exhausted, and food production drops.

Problems with Livestock

Overgrazing occurs when grazing animals eat all, or nearly all, the plants in an area. Many grasses can be partially eaten, but continue to grow. If they are eaten too much, however, they will die. The best pastureland in some countries has been taken over for farming. When animals graze on poorer land, overgrazing is more likely to occur. With less vegetation and ground cover, the likelihood of erosion and soil depletion increases.

A food crisis affects animals as well as people. Thin cows like these cannot fetch a good price at market.

Any rain that does fall on bare, hard ground tends to run off and is wasted rather than absorbed into the ground by root systems and rich, porous soil.

During a famine, livestock, like humans, suffer from a lack of food. Some livestock are sold or traded for other foods, but a very thin cow cannot command a high price. If the livestock are not slaughtered, they often die of disease or malnutrition. This means that when conditions improve, many families do not have any remaining livestock to breed and replenish the herd.

A boy watches a swarm of locusts eat a field in Mauritania. A locust, a kind of grasshopper, can eat its weight in food each day.

And they may be too poor to buy new animals.

Locusts

Locusts are a kind of grasshopper. They are usually solitary creatures. When there are too many in one place, however, they form swarms of millions or even billions. A locust can eat its weight in food each day. A swarm of locusts can eat an entire field in just a few hours. Crop-destroying locusts have contributed to many food crises throughout history. They are controlled with pesticides, but the right pesticides and tools are not always immediately available when a swarm of locusts suddenly heads toward a farm.

Rural Living

Many people in Africa live in rural areas far from cities. In some places there are no roads, only dirt tracks. These villages don't have grocery stores with big delivery trucks that bring food from other places. They are entirely dependent on the food that their inhabitants are able to produce. If bad weather, locusts, or other problems damage livestock and crops, villagers usually don't have money to import food from other places. It's also hard for charities to get food to them. According to UNICEF, children in remote, rural areas are nearly twice as likely to be undernourished than those living in cities.

Undernutrition and Disease

Undernutrition is, of course, a result of a food crisis. But it can also make a food crisis worse. Many people in Africa live with chronic undernutrition. They have some food to eat, but not quite enough. Often, they are missing important nutrients. When a food crisis happens, they can become very undernourished very quickly.

Undernourished people have a difficult time working. They may move sluggishly or be too weak to perform physical labor. Hungry people find it hard to concentrate and learn new things. This makes it harder to earn money for food when crops fail.

Undernourishment also makes people more likely to become sick. The World Health Organization (WHO) estimates that one million people in Africa die from malaria each year. In sub-Saharan Africa, an estimated 25.8 million people are living with HIV, the virus that causes

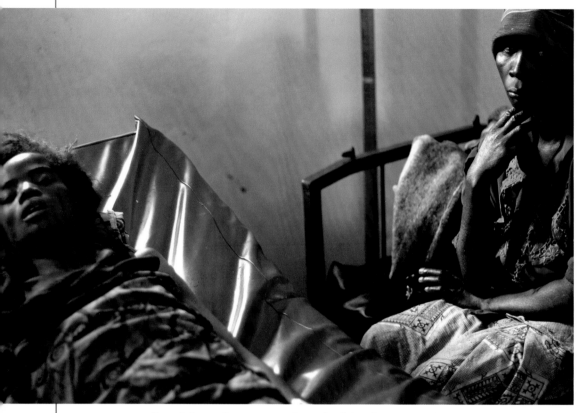

A woman lies dying of AIDS at a hospital in the Congo. Diseases such as AIDS and malaria can make a food crisis worse.

AIDS, according to the Joint United Nations Programme on HIV/AIDS.

Malaria, AIDS, and other diseases that are endemic to some African countries further weaken their victims, lowering productivity in those countries. Those who die often leave behind orphaned children or elderly parents who are unable to support themselves. Therefore, children and the elderly are more likely to be chronically undernourished.

Trade Barriers

African nations have been encouraged to plant cash crops to sell to other countries. But African agricultural products are not worth very much on the international market. Part of the problem is trade barriers in the form of tariffs and subsidies.

A tariff is a tax on materials or services that a country imports. A subsidy is money given by a government to a person or group to support a business that benefits the larger public or the national interest. Europe's Common Agricultural Policy places high tariffs on many imports from poor countries. At the same time, it offers subsidies to European farmers to export their produce. Many other developed nations have similar policies. These policies make it very hard for African farmers to sell their crops at a good price. African nations have demanded that other nations change their policies, but developed nations are reluctant to do so because they wish to protect their own farmers' interests.

Debt

Many African nations have developed huge debts to other nations. They borrowed money from developed countries and often from the World Bank. The World

Bank is an international organization that lends money to nations for projects related to economic development and poverty reduction. Some of these projects are very successful. Others are not. Regardless of the result, the borrowed money must be paid back. If nations don't make payments on their loans from the World Bank, then it will not lend money for new projects. Repaying the loans is thus a top priority for governments of developing countries. This means that nations have less or no money to feed people during a famine or to do things to prevent future famines.

Agricultural Self-Sufficiency

Most African countries do not produce enough food to feed all of their inhabitants. So, they must import food from other nations. This requires money, which African nations do not always have enough of. This can become a crisis when drought, locust infestations, or other problems cause crops to fail, increasing the amount of food that needs to be imported.

War

War can stimulate famine by forcing people to move off their land for safety. Civil war is a persistent problem in several African nations. Often, a particular ethnic or

Rebels gather along the Chad-Sudan border. Civil war disrupts agriculture and can interfere with the transport of food aid.

tribal group will control the government and may begin to oppress the other ethnic or tribal groups living in the country. These oppressed groups often form rebel armies and try to overthrow the ruling government. These civil wars can rage on for years, and each side often victimizes those who get caught in the middle and are just trying to make enough money or grow enough food to survive and avoid hunger.

Refugees are people who flee their homes because of natural disaster or war, or because the government does not approve of their religious or political beliefs.

Many end up in refugee camps that are set up by aid organizations. Refugee camps generally offer free food and medical care. But war can prevent donations from being delivered where they are needed. Fighting may block an important road, or government or rebel soldiers may steal the food. Refugees are not at home to tend their crops. Invading armies may eat the food out of untended fields. Or, the crops may simply die. The resulting scarcity of crops can worsen an already-serious food crisis.

Government

Democracy is a system of government in which the people vote for their leaders in regular elections. In a free press, newspapers, television, and other media make sure that people know what their leaders are doing. If a leader doesn't do what the people want, they will elect someone else. Because of this, democratically elected leaders work hard to prevent famines. A famine has never occurred in a functioning democracy with a free press.

Many African nations are not democracies. They are dictatorships. In a dictatorship, the leader is not elected and has complete power. Dictators restrict what the media can say and can threaten all critics with arrest, violence, or even murder. As a result, the power of dictators is usually not affected by food crises. This means that they can decide not to prepare for potential famines or take the necessary steps to lessen the effects once one is under way. Dictators can use money intended for food for other things, like strengthening the army and security forces or even building lavish palaces for their personal use. They have used hunger as a weapon to weaken rebels during civil war. They have ignored famines in their countries because they simply didn't care about the people who were starving.

Poverty

Most famine-stricken nations have some food supplies, but they are usually too expensive for poor people to buy. Whole families can starve, even if the market down the street is full. Poverty is where famines start and end. Drought, war, or other problems affect food production. People don't have enough money to buy the smaller and more expensive amounts of food that are available. They become more undernourished and sick. Food aid keeps them alive. Yet hunger, sickness, drought, and war make them poorer than they were before and more vulnerable to the next food crisis.

Twentieth-Century African Famines

The second half of the twentieth century saw many food crises and famines in Africa. Bad weather, unstable political situations, misguided development policies, and other factors led to food insecurity in many nations. The developed world did provide aid, but some development, humanitarian, and lending policies made the situations worse.

Nigeria, 1967–1969

Nigeria won its independence from England in 1960. However, the peoples of the former British colony were not unified. In the desert north, Muslim feudal states were semi-autonomous. In the south and east were Christian and Animist kingdoms. (Animism is a religion in which practitioners believe that individual spirits inhabit objects in nature.) In 1967, the nation broke out in civil war. The province of Biafra in southeastern Nigeria tried to establish itself as an independent nation.

The war provoked a famine in Biafra from 1967 to 1969 among the Igbo people, one of Nigeria's many ethnic groups. The central government used the famine as a weapon of war. It would not allow humanitarian aid into the region. Some agencies sneaked food and medical teams into Biafra at night, but their efforts weren't enough. The famine killed an estimated 1.5 million people, and Biafra did not gain independence from Nigeria. The Igbo people became one of Nigeria's most impoverished ethnic groups in the wake of the famine, the civil war, and post-war discrimination by the government.

The Sahel and Ethiopia, 1968–1973

In the 1950s and 1960s, rainfall was above average in the Sahel. This caused some people to rely too heavily on farming for their income. But in 1968, the amount of rainfall began to decrease, and by 1970 a drought was in effect. The drought was more severe in some Sahelian

In remote, famine-stricken areas, planes may drop packages of food aid. Here, nomads in the Sahel gather bran sticks dropped during the 1973 famine.

countries than in others. Niger, Mauritania, and Mali were the hardest hit.

In 1972, the United Nations began sending food aid. Also in 1972, bad weather reduced the grain harvests in Russia, India, and China. These nations are major producers and consumers of grain. At the same time, the United States had fields lying empty to prevent what had been expected grain surpluses. All of this resulted in a worldwide reduction—and scarcity in some places—of grain supplies, causing the price of grain to increase. In consequence, the United Nations couldn't send as much food aid to Africa in 1973 and 1974.

The Sahelian famine peaked in 1973, with an estimated 100,000 people dying from starvation that year. Almost all of the Sahelian countries had enough food to feed everyone if it had been divided equally. But the pastoralists and the farmers in the Sahel did not have money to buy food at market prices when their own crops failed. Mercifully, rainfall increased in 1974, finally ending the drought and the famine.

Drought hit parts of Ethiopia during the same period. Significant rain didn't fall in the Wollo and Tigre provinces of Ethiopia in 1972 and 1973, leading to crop failures. In March 1973, 1,500 farmers demonstrated in the capital, requesting aid. The government ignored them and downplayed the seriousness of the situation in general.

By August 1973, 60,000 rural refugees were packed into towns and refugee camps. In September, the dictator of Ethiopia, Emperor Haile Selassie, was removed from power. This allowed humanitarian aid to start arriving in October. Unfortunately, this was two months after the peak of the famine. An estimated 100,000 died, despite food being available in Ethiopian markets.

> *Significant rain didn't fall in the Wollo and Tigre provinces of Ethiopia in 1972 and 1973, leading to crop failures . . . By August 1973, 60,000 rural refugees were packed into towns and refugee camps . . . An estimated 100,000 died . . .*

People in the Wollo province of Ethiopia wait for food distribution during the 1973 famine.

Partly in response to the Sahel and Ethiopian famines, the United Nations World Food conference in 1974 brought together representatives of 135 nations. They wrote a Universal Declaration on the Eradication of Hunger and Malnutrition. It began, "Every man, woman, and child has the inalienable right to be free from hunger and malnutrition in order to develop fully and maintain their physical and mental faculties." The declaration spawned twenty resolutions regarding food crises, including policies to improve nutrition and seed industrial development. Yet famines continued to occur in Africa, despite the world's best intentions and resolutions.

Sudan, 1983–1988

Sudan is another African country in which peoples of many different religions, cultures, and ethnicities coexist, and not always peacefully. Muslim Arabs inhabit the desert in the north, Black Africans live in the south, and mixed tribes live in the middle. Sudan gained independence from England in 1956. In the 1960s, it implemented large-scale sorghum and sesame farming in non-desert areas. This was bad for peasants and pastoralists who farmed and raised livestock using traditional methods. Many lost their land and had to make do with inferior land. As a result, many local, small-scale farmers moved to the cities to be laborers. The country was also engaged in civil war from 1955 to 1972. The war raged between the predominantly Muslim north, where the central government was located, and the south, which was mainly Black and Christian or Animist.

Oil was discovered in southern Sudan in 1978. After a decade of uneasy peace, civil war broke out again in 1983, coinciding with a drought and provoking a famine from 1983 to 1985. After drought conditions improved, the government decided to use famine as a weapon in the war. Local militias supported by the central government destroyed crops and prevented food from reaching the rebellious southern areas. The famine was intended to punish the ethnic groups who were in opposition to the central government and to force them from their oil-rich land. Food aid was mostly handed out in refugee camps in Ethiopia to the east and in towns far from the land the government wanted. This strategy was successful, for most people vacated the oil-rich territory the central government coveted.

Many victims of famine and civil war end up in refugee camps. Here refugees from the Tigre province of Ethiopia gather at a refugee camp in Sudan.

Ethiopia, 1984–1986, 1988

A severe drought hit Ethiopia in the early 1980s before the country had fully recovered from the famine of the 1970s. Famine again struck several Ethiopian provinces in 1984. The international community provided aid, but civil war made delivery of food difficult. Two provinces, Tigre (in the south) and Eritrea (in the far north), were fighting against the central government. By late 1984, the Tigre People's

Liberation Forces and the Relief Society of Tigre controlled most of Tigre.

Farmers and rural residents had two options. The first was to turn to the central government and go to a city for famine relief. But the government often only handed out food to people who belonged to certain political associations of which they approved. The government was also stealing food aid and giving it to soldiers.

The second option was to flee the country. The Relief Society of Tigre led 170,000 people to neighboring Sudan between November 1984 and April 1985. Several refugee camps were set up across the border. But most people returned to their land within a few months, hoping the rains would come and they could plant their crops. Instead, the drought spread. In 1986, a plague of locusts made the problem even worse.

The government tried to resettle 600,000 peasants from the north in the south, hoping to quell the rebellion down there. The government also tried to move peasants into planned villages with water, schools, and medical facilities. Many peasants chose to flee rather than move, however. An estimated one million people died in Ethiopia during this famine.

Conditions improved briefly, but drought caused another famine in Ethiopia in 1988. About six million people were at risk of starvation. Strikingly, trucks of

American and United Nations troops stationed in Somalia in the early
1990s helped ensure that food aid reached famine victims.

food aid passed trucks of locally grown food leaving the
famine-stricken area for other places. While the famine
victims were poor, other people still had money to buy
food. Merchants could have given away the food instead
of selling it. But then they would have risked being
famine victims, too.

The continuing civil war made getting aid shipments
to those who needed them difficult. In addition, similar
conflicts in neighboring countries caused refugees to
stream into Ethiopia. These refugees needed food as
well, creating a heavier burden for the country. Periodic

droughts and conflicts have caused Ethiopia to remain food insecure to this day.

Somalia, 1992

In 1991, the twenty-two-year reign of Somali dictator Siad Barre ended. Conflict then broke out in Somalia where various clans and other groups had been contending against each other for several years. The violence became more widespread as different groups tried to gain power, and the food-supply network was disrupted. Battles and theft of seeds prevented planting. Soldiers took crops to feed themselves. Tractors and irrigation pumps were also stolen. Many people left their homes for safety. This led to a smaller harvest than usual. The violence made importing food from other nations difficult. Food prices in cities rose. A famine occurred.

About two million people faced starvation. From 1992 to 1994, American troops and United Nations peacekeepers delivered food and tried to prevent violence. The local food supply gradually increased, but conflict still continued to occur. Even today, Somalia does not have a functional government.

Food crises of different sizes continued to occur throughout Africa in the 1990s and into the new millennium. The next chapter will look at some food crises currently occurring in Africa.

Current Famines in Africa

Currently, food crises are occurring in West Africa and East Africa. In May 2006, the USAID Famine Early Warning System Network listed seven countries with food emergencies, three nations with alerts, and two with watches. All were in these two African regions. Indeed, it seems that a food crisis is always occurring somewhere in Africa.

West Africa

The recent food crisis in West Africa affected the nations of Niger, Mali, Mauritania, and

Burkina Faso. This section will focus on Niger because it experienced the largest famine.

Niger is an extremely poor country. In 2004, it suffered a severe drought and an invasion by locusts. This devastated the country's crops and led to famine in 2005. The regions of Tahoua, Maradi, and Zinder were hit hardest. More than 80 percent of Niger is desert. Crops cannot grow there. The country must depend on non-desert land for its food. As such, when a harvest fails, it quickly becomes a major problem.

Like many African nations, Niger has rainy and dry seasons. Usually, August is the wettest month. But in August 2004, hardly any rain fell, and many crops died. Then for two months, swarms of locusts ate Niger's crops. That October's harvest was one of the smallest in years. Niger had built up emergency food reserves after the famines of the 1970s and 1980s, but these reserves had been allowed to dwindle.

In November 2004, the United Nations began asking member countries for aid for Niger. Few nations offered any help. Nevertheless, in February 2005, the United Nations World Food Programme started providing emergency aid for 400,000 people. In May, it asked member nations for aid once again. But by June, the UN hadn't received any pledges of help.

The government of Niger tried to pretend that the problem wasn't very serious or extensive. It offered

A farmer in Niger points at his dry field. In recent years, Niger and neighboring countries have suffered food crises due to drought and locusts.

bags of millet, which is similar to rice, to affected farmers at low prices. Many farmers still couldn't afford it. Even though the government was ignoring the problem, local journalists were not. They were accused of being unpatriotic when they began to report on the problem.

In June, 2,000 people demanded free food as they marched through the streets of Niamey, the capital of Niger. The government claimed it could not afford to hand out free food. The protesters responded that the government knew there would be a shortage of food, but did nothing to prepare for it.

In July, people began to flee the country. Some of those who stayed ate only one meal per day. Others ate wild plants because they didn't have anything else to eat. Livestock also died from lack of food. In mid-July, the World Food Programme began helping 800,000 people in addition to the 400,000 it had been feeding since February. Other relief organizations also provided food and medical care. The government of Niger esti-mated that at least 3.5 million people didn't have enough to eat.

In July 2005, people began to flee Niger. Some of those who stayed ate only one meal per day. Others ate wild plants because they didn't have any-thing else to eat. Livestock also died from lack of food.

The United Nations again asked for money to help with the crisis. Photos of starving children had since appeared on television and in newspapers worldwide. In response, the UN received $10 million in donations, even though it had originally asked for $30 million. By then, many people had died of starvation.

Although governments and aid organizations blamed each other for the crisis, Niger's social struc-tures were partly to blame as well. Most men in Niger are polygamous, which means they have more than one wife. Each wife has a small plot of land for growing vegetables. The women also work in larger family fields, but men control access to the grain from these fields.

Food crises make people more likely to become sick. Here workers unload medicine from France intended for famine victims in Niger.

During the famine in Niger, some men left their villages to look for work or food. They often left grain in locked storage. The women and children left behind were undernourished, even though the family technically had food. It just wasn't accessible. The men may have assumed that their families would receive humanitarian aid. In some cases, they were right. They may have also been saving the grain for more difficult times later.

In August 2005, rains swept across West Africa. The FAO provided seeds to farmers. Spraying with insecticide had reduced the threat of locusts. In spring 2006, Niger had a good grain harvest, and food access had improved in some regions. However, many parts of Niger were still food insecure because grain prices were high, food reserves were empty, and there was a lack of milk. The United Nations and USAID estimated that 1.8 million people in Niger would face moderate or severe food insecurity in 2006.

East Africa

A food crisis is also currently occurring in East Africa. People in the nations of Ethiopia, Kenya, Djibouti, and Somalia are facing starvation because of drought and conflict. Drought has hit different parts of the four nations since 1999. Ethiopia has suffered five major droughts in the last twenty years. Families and entire regions are often unable to recover from one crisis before another one begins.

Drought in Kenya has affected animals as well as people, killing much of the livestock.

In April 2006, the United Nations estimated that 15 million people in East Africa had been affected by the drought. Northern and eastern Kenya, for example, have experienced three years of drought beginning in 2003. In November 2005, it rained for only a day and a half in the Wajir region of Kenya. At that time of year, it usually rains for two weeks straight. The drought has particularly affected pastoralist communities. No rain means no grasses and other plants for animals to graze on. Many people moved away from their usual pastures. Others stayed and watched their animals die.

In western Kenya, however, farmers had a huge crop of maize in early 2006. The government ordered farmers to sell their crops. The government would then distribute the grain to famine-stricken areas. Yet the government offered only credit notes to the farmers, rather than cash. Meanwhile, businessmen from Tanzania offered the Kenyan farmers cash. The businessmen then sold the grain to people in Malawi and Zambia, countries that were also experiencing food shortages. The Kenyan farmers wanted to sell their grain for cash, not credit notes. As a result, many of them refused to sell to their own government, and fellow Kenyans suffered as a consequence.

Rain began falling in Kenya in spring 2006, but that did not end the crisis. Crops need months to grow before they can be harvested, much less be processed into food products. In addition, heavy rains on hard, sun-baked earth caused flooding in some areas. This forced people to move off their land. Rain-damaged roads also prevented food aid from reaching many communities.

The famine situation is also severe in Somalia. The country has not had an effective central government since its last food crisis, which was in 1992. The current government controls only a small part of the country. It and two other groups are fighting for control. Armed militias roam the countryside, killing villagers. Many people have moved away from their land because they are afraid of the violence. Fighting broke out in the capital, Mogadishu, in May 2006.

The civil war has made it difficult for food aid to reach people who need it. Militias often capture trucks carrying food into the countryside. The food thus feeds the soldiers and not the starving peasants. Some villagers who can't get food aid are surviving by eating leaves. Spring rains also caused flooding in some parts of Somalia, making many roads impassable to aid workers.

The World Food Programme has asked for more than $500 million to help starving people in East Africa. More than half of the money is for Somalia. Unfortunately, violence may make it impossible to get the food to those who need it. Clearly, more must be done to prevent famines. The following chapter will look at some strategies to do just this.

Strategies to Combat Famine

5

I n 2001, eighteen African countries faced food emergencies. According to the UN Food and Agriculture Organization:

- Eight of these nations were involved in internal conflicts;
- Three were trying to recover from conflicts, in particular dealing with many refugees and internally displaced persons;
- And seven had been affected by natural disasters such as floods, cyclones, or

drought, and/or couldn't afford to import food to prevent shortages.

Conflict, climate, and poverty—all three are crucial in sparking and sustaining famines. Currently, many people are working to reduce famine in Africa and around the world. Here are some strategies people are trying:

Famine Early Warning Systems

Organizations such as USAID have created famine early warning systems. People in the United States and Africa monitor information about the weather, how well crops are growing, and the health of pastures. Carefully examining this information can give early warning of droughts, potential crop failures, and overgrazing. Countries and aid organizations can then take steps to avoid a food crisis. They will also be more prepared to provide food aid if it is needed.

Local Food Aid

Many aid agencies now buy food from the nation experiencing a famine to give to the victims. This helps provide food relief while simultaneously supporting that nation's agriculture (rather than importing food from other countries). It also reduces food transportation and delivery time, so hungry people get fed sooner. If the famine-stricken nation does not have any or enough food, grain may still be bought from neighboring countries.

Work-for-Food Programs

Some countries have instituted work-for-food programs in an attempt to reduce the effects and likelihood of widespread famine. Instead of simply receiving humanitarian aid, people experiencing food insecurity can earn money by working on useful projects that may help reduce the insecurity. For example, Ethiopia's Productive Safety Net Programme provides food aid or cash to residents of chronically food-insecure communities. In return, people perform labor on public works projects in their communities. These may include building roads and bridges, reclaiming damaged land, renovating schools and health-care facilities, and improving access to irrigation and drinking water. These public works are intended to reduce the likelihood that the community will experience famine in the future. Many other developing nations have similar programs.

Traditional Agriculture

Some communities in developing nations are turning away from the agricultural methods suggested to them by developed nations. These include devoting huge fields to a single crop and the use of chemical fertilizers, pesticides, and mechanical devices such as tractors. More Africans are planting like their ancestors did. They alternate small plots of different crops, reducing the risk of pest infestation and soil depletion. They grow plants that are native to Africa and are better adapted to wet and dry seasons. This type of agriculture may be more likely to yield food, even during a drought.

Genetically Modified Crops

Genetically modified (GM) organisms are living things that contain genes transplanted from other living things. These genes give plants new characteristics. Crops may be genetically engineered to be more nutritious or to grow better in dry conditions.

Some people doubt the ability of biotechnology to reduce starvation. Many genetically engineered crops require large amounts of chemical fertilizers and pesticides to grow in African soils and climates. These chemicals can pollute water and do not give anything back to the soil that will make it fertile year to year. It's also unclear whether African nations could sell GM crops.

Many European nations, in particular, are very suspicious of GM crops. Most people there won't buy GM foods. Since many African nations export their crops to

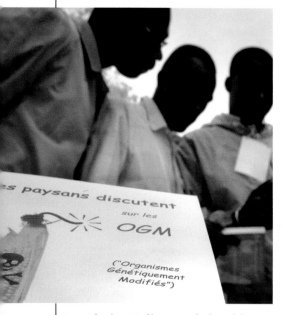

People in Mali consult booklets about genetically modified organisms. GM crops and organisms are viewed with skepticism in many areas of the world.

Europe, they don't want to plant GM crops if there's no demand for them. They are also reluctant to accept GM food aid. Countries worry that people might plant some of the GM grain they received as aid. This could get mixed in with non-GM grain and threaten European sales of even non-modified grain. In 2002, Zimbabwe accepted GM corn food aid from the United States on the condition that it be ground before entering the country. That way, the food aid would still reach people, but the corn couldn't accidentally be planted. Other nations have similar policies. Genetically modified organisms must overcome these and other hurdles before they begin to reduce famine.

Better Water

In 2002, more than one billion people didn't have access to clean water, according to the World Health Organization. That included 42 percent of the people in sub-Saharan Africa. Increasing the number of people with safe sources of drinking water will reduce disease. This will make them

A worker opens an irrigation tap at a rice research center in the Ivory Coast. Better use of irrigation could reduce the number and severity of famines.

more productive workers and, therefore, less likely to be poor. And reducing poverty reduces famines.

Better use of water in agriculture can also decrease the likelihood of famine. Proper watering of crops lessens soil erosion. Excess water from irrigation can be collected and used again. Lining irrigation channels or using pipes can reduce the amount of water needed. Of course, much of African agriculture depends solely on rain. Tanks and reservoirs can be used to capture rain-water during the wet season and store it during the dry season. This can help ensure healthy crops.

Reduce Conflict

One reason why Africa continues to have famines is because it continues to experience violent conflicts. Nations need to learn how to resolve their differences without resorting to violence, whether the conflict is within or across borders. One possibility is to strengthen the World Court so that it can settle problems before strife occurs. Violence is also less likely to happen in democratic countries because people have a voice in their government. Establishing democracies in more African nations could help reduce the number of conflicts and famines.

Money that nations at war spend on guns is money not spent on agriculture, health, education, and other areas that can help prevent famine. Warring groups in Africa usually do not make their own weapons. They buy guns from developed nations, including the United States. One way to reduce conflicts would be for developed nations to stop selling weapons to developing countries. Without guns and bullets, fighting a war is considerably more challenging.

Food Security

The Food and Agriculture Organization of the United Nations conducts a Special Programme for Food Security. It works with nations and regional economic organizations to draw up plans to increase food security in developing nations. Donors to the program provide money for projects. The plans often incorporate ideas discussed in this chapter, including work-for-food programs and planting more diverse crops.

Free elections and a democratic government can reduce the likelihood of famine and war in a nation.

Nigeria has already seen some success from its National Program for Food Security, which began in 2000. A partnership with China has brought experts to Nigeria to assist with building and repairing irrigation systems, dams, and other water control systems. Farming of crops such as rice, yams, millet, and vegetables has increased. The program significantly improved food security at the test sites.

No one program will eliminate famine in Africa. The network of cause and effect is too large and complex. Yet each improvement in the way things are done, no matter how small, has the potential to save human life. With investments of time, money, and knowledge—and the concern, commitment, and cooperation of the world's wealthy nations—perhaps famine will one day become a thing of the past.

Glossary

cash crop Crops that are planted for export rather than local use.

debt An amount of money owed to another person or organization.

developing nations Countries that are poor, contain only a little industry, and score low on the United Nations' Human Development Index.

drought An extended period of time with little or no rain.

erosion The process of wearing away the surface of the earth by wind or water.

famine A widespread shortage of food that leaves many people hungry, even starving.

genetically modified (GM) organism A living thing that contains genetic material transplanted from a different living thing.

irrigation A way to provide water to dry farmland through ditches or pipes.

pastoralist A person who raises livestock by moving to different grazing pastures at different times of the year.

subsidy Money given by a government to a person or group in support of a business that is a benefit to the public and/or national interest.

tariff A tax on materials or services that a country imports.

For More Information

CARE Headquarters
151 Ellis Street
Atlanta, GA 30303
(404) 681-2552
Web site: http://www.care.org

Food and Agriculture Organization of the United Nations
Liaison Office for North America (LOWA)
2175 K Street NW, Suite 300
Washington, DC 20437-0001
(202) 653-2400
Web site: http://www.fao.org

International Food Policy Research Institute
2033 K Street NW
Washington, DC 20006-1002
(202) 862-5600
Web site: http://www.ifpri.org

Oxfam America
26 West Street
Boston, MA 02111
(800) 77-OXFAM
Web site: http://www.oxfamamerica.org

United States Fund for UNICEF
333 East 38th Street
New York, NY 10016
(212) 686-5522
(800) 4UNICEF (486-4233)
Web site: http://www.unicefusa.org

World Food Programme
Two United Nations Plaza
Room DC 2-2500
New York, NY 10017
(212) 963-8364
Web site: http://www.wfp.org/english

World Health Organization
Avenue Appia 20
1211 Geneva 27
Switzerland
Web site: http://www.who.int/en

Web Sites

Due to the changing nature of Internet links, Rosen Publishing has developed an online list of Web sites related to the subject of this book. This site is updated regularly. Please use this link to access the list:

http://www.rosenlinks.com/in/staf

For Further Reading

Berg, Elizabeth. *Ethiopia*. Milwaukee, WI: Gareth Stevens Publishing, 2000.

Bowden, Rob. *World Poverty*. Chicago, IL: Raintree, 2003.

Connolly, Sean. *Famine and Drought*. North Mankato, MN: Smart Apple Media, 2005.

Heinrichs, Ann. *Niger*. New York, NY: Children's Press, 2001.

Maddocks, Steven. *World Hunger*. Milwaukee, WI: World Almanac Books, 2004.

Mason, Paul. *Poverty*. Chicago, IL: Heinemann Library, 2006.

Murray, Jocelyn, and Sean Sheehan. *Africa*. New York, NY: Facts on File, 2003.

Oppong, Joseph R. *Africa South of the Sahara*. New York, NY: Chelsea House, 2005.

Walker, Jane. *Famine, Drought, and Plagues*. North Mankato, MN: Stargazer Books, 2004.

Bibliography

Aksoy, M. Ataman, and John C. Beghin, eds. *Global Agricultural Trade and Developing Countries.* Washington, DC: The International Bank for Reconstruction and Development/The World Bank, 2005.

Andersson, Hilary. "Niger's Children Continue Dying." BBC News. 2005. Retrieved May 4, 2006 (http://news.bbc.co.uk/1/hi/world/africa/4274728.stm).

Barou, Idy. "Bringing Relief to Niger's Hungry." BBC News. 2005. Retrieved May 4, 2006 (http://news.bbc.co.uk/1/hi/world/africa/4675379.stm).

Collins, Robert O., ed. *Problems in the History of Modern Africa.* Princeton, NJ: Marcus Wiener Publishers, 1997.

Heiden, David. *Dust to Dust: A Doctor's View of Famine in Africa.* Philadelphia, PA: Temple University Press, 1992.

"A History of Famine in Africa." BBC News. 1998. Retrieved May 4, 2006 (http://news.bbc.co.uk/1/hi/world/africa/86443.stm).

Keene, David. "Making Famine in Sudan." Environmental News Network. 1999. Retrieved May 11, 2006 (http://www.ennonline.net/fex/06/sf6.html).

"Kenya Farmers Reject Famine Plan." BBC News. 2006. Retrieved May 11, 2006 (http://news.bbc.co.uk/2/hi/africa/4602770.stm).

Kutzner, Patricia L. *World Hunger: A Reference Handbook.* Santa Barbara, CA: ABC-CLIO, 1991.

McCann, James C. "Climate and Causation in African History." *International Journal of African Historical Studies.* Vol. 32, No. 2–3, 1999, pp. 261–279.

McGovern, George. *The Third Freedom: Ending Hunger in Our Time.* New York, NY: Simon and Schuster, 2001.

Mynott, Adam. "Hunger and Misery Ravage Kenya." BBC News. 2006. Retrieved May 11, 2006 (http://news.bbc.co.uk/2/hi/africa/4598172.stm).

"Niger Scorns 'Free Food' Demands." BBC News. 2005. Retrieved May 4, 2006. (http://news.bbc.co.uk/1/hi/world/africa/4607345.stm).

"No Food Aid as Hungry Flee Niger." BBC News. 2005. Retrieved May 4, 2006 (http://news.bbc.co.uk/1/hi/world/africa/4655225.stm).

Okello, Benson. *A History of East Africa.* Kampala, Uganda: Fountain Publishers Ltd., 2002.

Rodale, Robert. *Save Three Lives: A Plan for Famine Prevention.* San Francisco, CA: Sierra Club Books, 1991.

Seager, Ashley, and Ewen MacAskill. "Africa Tells West: Scrap Trade Barriers." *Guardian.* 2005. Retrieved May 9, 2006 (http://business.guardian.co.uk/story/0,3604,1522243,00.html).

Sen, Amartya. *Poverty and Famines: An Essay on Entitlement and Deprivation.* Oxford, England: Clarendon Press, 1982.

Somerville, Keith. "Why Famine Stalks Africa." BBC News. 2002. Retrieved May 4, 2006 (http://news.bbc.co.uk/1/hi/world/africa/2449527.stm).

Suliman, Mohamed. "Civil War in Sudan: The Impact of Ecological Degradation." University of Pennsylvania African Studies Center. 1994. Retrieved May 9, 2006 (http://www.africa.upenn.edu/Articles_Gen/cvlw_env_sdn.html).

Thomson, Mike. "The Dangers of Taking Food Aid to Somalia." BBC News. 2006. Retrieved May 11, 2006 (http://news.bbc.co.uk/1/hi/world/africa/4966352.stm).

United Nations. *Report of the World Food Conference*, Rome, 5–16 November, 1974. New York, NY: United Nations, 1975.

United Nations. *United Nations Millennium Declaration*. New York, NY: United Nations, 2000.

United Nations Children's Fund. *Progress for Children: A Report Card on Nutrition*. No. 4. New York, NY: UNICEF Division of Communication, 2006.

United Nations Development Programme. *Human Development Report 2005*. New York, NY: United Nations, 2005.

"UN Seeks East Africa Drought Aid." BBC News. 2006. Retrieved May 11, 2006 (http://news.bbc.co.uk/1/hi/world/africa/4886608.stm).

Index

A

Africa
  colonialism in, 13–14, 30–31, 35
  continuing Western influence on,
    11–12, 14–16, 25–26, 41, 43, 49,
    51–52, 54
  current famines in, 40–47
  geography of, 7–10
  and slave trade, 12–13
  traditional agricultural practices
    in, 10–12, 35, 50–51

C

cash crops, 14, 16, 25

D

debts, 16, 25

E

erosion, 19, 20, 53
Ethiopian famines, 33–34,
    36–39, 45

F

famine
  climate causes, 18–19, 30, 31–33,
    47, 48
  definition of, 5
  and disease, 5, 21, 23–24, 29
  farming causes, 19–22, 26, 30,
    35–36, 41, 44, 51
  and the media, 28, 42, 43
  other words for, 5

political causes, 15, 25–29, 30, 35,
    36–37, 39, 44, 47, 48, 54
  strategies to combat, 6, 34, 48–55
Food and Agriculture Organization
    (FAO), 5, 44, 48, 54
food security, 6, 17, 18, 54–55

G

genetically modified (GM)
    organisms, 51–52

H

Human Development Index, 5

I

irrigation, 19, 39, 50, 53, 55

M

malnutrition, 21, 34

N

Nigerian famine (1967–1969), 30–31

P

pastoralists, 10, 16, 33, 35, 46
pesticides, 14, 16, 22, 51

S

Sahelian famine (1968–1973),
    31–34
Somalian famine (1992), 39, 47

subsidies, 25
Sudanese famine (1983–1988), 35–36

T
tariffs, 25

U
UNICEF, 4, 6, 23

USAID, 40, 44, 49

W
work-for-food programs, 50, 55
World Food Programme (WFP), 4,
    41, 43, 47
World Health Organization (WHO),
    23, 52

About the Author

Linley Erin Hall is a writer and editor in San Francisco, California. She has a B.S. degree in chemistry from Harvey Mudd College and a certificate in science communication from the University of California, Santa Cruz. She has written and edited several books for Rosen on issues relevant to drought and famine, including climate, the environment, and biotechnology.

Photo Credits

Cover (top left), p. 48 (bottom) © Gianluigi Guercia/AFP/Getty Images; cover (top right), p. 4 (bottom) © Mike Goldwater/Christian Aid/Getty Images; cover (bottom), pp. 3 (right), 4 (top) © Joel Robine/AFP/Getty Images; pp. 3 (left), 17 (top), 27 © Daniel Pepper/Getty Images; pp. 4 (middle), 42, 53, 55 © Issouf Sanogo/AFP/Getty Images; p. 7 Library of Congress Geography and Map Division; p. 9 (left) © Carsten Peter/National Geographic/Getty Images; p. 9 (middle) © Jose Azel/Aurora/Getty Images; p. 9 (right) ©Tim Graham/ Getty Images; p. 13 Library of Congress Rare Book and Special Collections Division; pp. 15, 40 (top) © Simon Maina/AFP/Getty Images; pp. 17 (middle), 30 (middle), 38 © Alexander Joe/AFP/Getty Images; pp. 17 (bottom), 24 © Spencer Platt/Getty Images; p. 19 © Jacob Silberberg/Getty Images; p. 21 © AP/Wide World Photos; p. 22 © G Diana/AFP/Getty Images; p. 30 (top) © Eric Cabanis/AFP/Getty Images; p. 30 (bottom) © Peter Jansson/AFP/Getty Images; p. 32 © Alain Nogues/Corbis Sygma; p. 34 ©Thomas Hoepker/ Magnum Photos; p. 36 ©William Betsch/AFP/Getty Images; p. 40 (middle, bottom) © AFP/Getty Images; p. 44 © Stephane de Sakutin/AFP/Getty Images; p. 45 ©Tony Karumba/AFP/Getty Images; p. 48 (top) © Nicolas Germain/AFP/Getty Images; p. 48 (middle) ©Thomas Mukoya/AFP/Getty Images; p. 52 © Jean-Philippe Ksiazek/AFP/Getty Images.

Designer: Tom Forget; Photo Researcher: Amy Feinberg